SURROUNDED
BY SIN
GROUNDED
BY LOVE

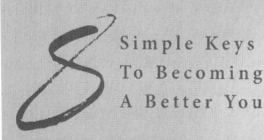

Simple Keys
To Becoming
A Better You

TAMBRA CHERIE

First printing 2018

The book was Edited by Julia Beverly

Scriptures taken from New International Version (NIV)
Application Life Study Bible.

A PERSONAL MESSAGE

This book is dedicated to my parents and grandparents. You are the essence and epitome of who I am. The perfect blend. Thank you for your guidance, patience, love, strength and commitment. To all my family, friends, and loved ones, thank you for loving me just the way I am and for who I am. To my nephew Priest, you are the perfect example of perfection and strength. To my nephew Keegan, know that Tee-Tee loves you unconditionally. To my radio family, colleagues, and mentors, thank you for always being there, and for giving me an opportunity and a platform to do what I love. To all my listeners and supporters, thank you for all your love and support throughout the years. May God continue to bless all of you beyond your own imaginations.

With much love and gratitude,

Tambra Cherie

PREFACE

    I believe that God has a predestined plan for each and every one of you. With this book, I hope to inspire, encourage, and motivate you to fulfill God's plan and become the best version of yourself. My goal is to help you find purpose in your pain, discernment in your disappointments, and peace within your chaos. I want to encourage you to grow throughout life's disappointments and challenges by embracing a new perspective. Amidst all the lessons I've learned on my own journey of becoming a better version of myself, I've given God all the glory. By sharing my own experiences, I hope to inspire you to take a deeper look within yourself and embrace your truth.

*Listen, my son,
to your father's
instruction and do not
forsake your
mother's teaching. They will
be a garland to grace your
head and a chain to adorn
your neck.*

– Proverbs 1:8-9

INTRODUCTION

The Self-Analysis

The room was filled with loud music, attractive people, rich celebrities, successful entrepreneurs, and enough marijuana and liquor to put an entire community under the influence. I was young, vibing to the music. I felt important, partying behind closed doors with music moguls, successful athletes, producers, and entertainers. In the entertainment business, this is what we're all working towards, right?

As I sat there, all I could do was think. I had an honest conversation with myself, and that night, in that very room, I realized that this was not the goal I was working towards nor the reputation I wanted to gain. I love entertainment and I am beyond thankful for the career God has blessed me with. However, it was then I learned the importance of staying grounded. I realized how easy it was to get sucked into the dark side of the industry and its seemingly alluring lifestyle.

That same night, a home girl called and asked me if I had ever tried Ecstasy. She had just moved to Atlanta, and I had brought her around some of those same successful artists, rappers, and entertainers in a previous engagement. Nonetheless, my answer was no, and I didn't plan on trying any. She went on to explain how a popular rapper/actor had asked if she would join him and his girl-friend at the time in a more intimate setting. She told me she walked in on about ten people in bed, but she didn't participate.

I was surprised by her story because I had been around those same individuals for a while, as I was a correspondent for a very popular Hip-Hop website in the industry at the time. These individuals had never approached me with requests for those type of activities. Matter of fact, there were a couple of occasions when we all partied together, and I would see them again in the studio as it was back to business.

Later, someone who worked for the record label explained to me why I hadn't been invited to those after-hours activities. He said that it was my demeanor and the way I carried myself. He shared with me that I'd always been treated with respect because of the way I handled business and commanded a room. They knew I was there to work. They knew I was on a mission. I would always come in with a smile, but I would get right to the business at hand.

People treat you how you allow them to treat you. The way you carry yourself tells a lot about your character without you even opening your mouth. Always choose character over conformity, no matter what's going on around you. That night, I prayed, and I thanked God. I thanked God for the things He was doing in my life. I thanked Him for giving me praying parents, and I thanked Him for the morals and values they instilled within me. As kids, we don't always understand the reasons for the rules our parents put in place, but the lessons they gave me have stayed with me for a lifetime. I thanked God for helping me grow.

Most importantly, I thanked God for His timing. There are some things we simply cannot handle early on in life. Sometimes, we want things that we might not be ready for yet. You might be questioning yourself, wondering why you're still living in the same city, or still working that boring job? You may question why you didn't get a certain job when you know you were well qualified for the position. You may question why a relationship didn't work out even though you gave it your best.

Instead of looking at life's disappointments as missed opportunities, learn to view them as blessings. When something is blocked, it's blocked for a reason. It may not be your season, or you may not be ready for the weather the season will produce. How will you feel when it rains, and you don't have an umbrella, a coat, or even a piece of clothing to protect you from it? You get wet. Not only do you get wet, but days later you get sick. When you get sick, you get weak. Not only can this sickness potentially harm you, but it can break you. You weren't prepared for the storm. You weren't prepared for the rain. You're weren't prepared for the season. If God has blocked something from your life, there's a reason.

So, you may say, you've been working hard and doing everything you need to do for that promotion, but it still hasn't come. Maybe the promotion isn't for you- maybe it's time for you to leave that job altogether and start that business you've always wanted to start?

Perhaps you've been in the same relationship for years and are starting to wonder if you'll ever get married. You start to question yourself. There is a reason why you're not someone's husband or wife. Some of you are waiting on God and God is waiting on you.

Ladies, some of you don't care to cook or clean for yourselves, let alone for someone else. Men, are you ready to be the head of a household, the provider and leader of a family? Are you ready to be faithful?

Are you tired of making the same mistakes over and over? These things take time and many who think they are prepared are not. That's why it's been blocked. It didn't work out because it wasn't the right time or season.

Maybe you still have some growing to do. Think about it. Would you rather marry the man or woman of your dreams now and have the marriage end in divorce seven years later, or instead marry the man or woman of your dreams seven years from now and have a marriage that lasts until the end of time? We all tend to want things we may not be ready for. Your attitude isn't ready. Your patience runs short. You can't control your tongue. We live in a world where we must have everything right now. We push for our timing instead of trusting God's timing.

You must recognize the blocked plays in your life and acknowledge them. Is it really the play or the player? Ask yourself how can you grow where you are to help become the person you want or need to be?

Start by doing a thorough self-analysis. It's easy to have strong opinions and be critical when analyzing other people but try applying those same methods to your own life. Accept constructive criticism. Be honest with yourself.

What do you feel has been blocked in your life? Are there any disappointments in your life that you can be thankful for today? Is there a relationship in your past that didn't work out but looking back you realize it was a blessing?

Take the time to answer these questions and write them down in the space provided. You may realize that things didn't happen according to your plan because you were not truly ready or prepared for the results.

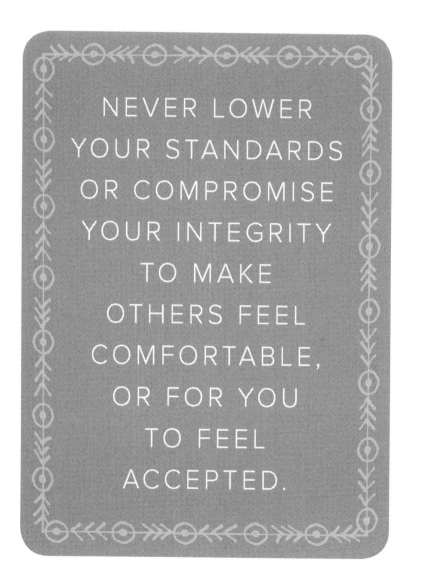

NEVER LOWER
YOUR STANDARDS
OR COMPROMISE
YOUR INTEGRITY
TO MAKE
OTHERS FEEL
COMFORTABLE,
OR FOR YOU
TO FEEL
ACCEPTED.

Let your conversation be always full of grace, seasoned with salt, so that you know how to answer everyone.

— Colossians 4:6

CHAPTER 1

Never Settle • Set Boundaries

I often meet ladies who long for a relationship or companionship so much that they'll ultimately settle for a piece of a man rather than no man at all. The same is true for some men when it comes to women. But settling for less than you deserve will affect you negatively in the long run.

Never settle for anything in life; not in business, and not in relationships. I've always considered myself a relationship-type of female, and every man in my life has pretty much treated me like a queen because that's the only thing I accepted. People truly treat you the way you allow them to treat you. If you hold a person to a higher standard, that person will ultimately step up if they want to keep you in their life.

You determine how you want to be treated. Whatever you allow, good or bad, will continue. For example, I have never dated a man who didn't open the car door for me. Not because that's what he automatically did upon dating, but because that's what I asked of him upon the initial date, and that continued throughout the relationship. If a person cannot treat you the way you feel like you should be treated, then learn to move on or don't allow that person to play a significant role in your life.

However, you must clearly communicate to other people how you would like to be treated, whether in a relationship or in a workplace. You shouldn't assume that anyone knows what you want. Set boundaries early on. Clearly communicate your deal breakers in all relationships, whether business or personal. Keep an open line of communication and express your desires clearly in a way that isn't controlling. Simply let the other person know how you would like to be treated, and make sure they understand. In any relationship, you have the choice to voice what you will or will not accept from an individual. This can be done with much respect and diligence.

What are your deal breakers in relationships, friendships, or business? For example, if your significant other cheats on you, this may be a deal breaker in the relationship. Your significant other should know upfront that cheating is unacceptable. This is something that should be communicated and not assumed by either party.

Communication is essential for all relationships, but you must learn how to effectively communicate with others. Communication is a skill and it takes genuine effort to not only learn how to convey your message clearly, but master the tone in which you share the information. I've watched friendships, partnerships, and even relationships fail drastically because one party could not deliver the message in the proper tone. When communicating, it's imperative to learn to talk with each other, and not at each other or over one another. Don't just hear the words, but listen to the message, regardless if you agree or disagree. Create dialogue and learn the value of respecting one's thoughts, feelings, concerns, and opinions.

Learn to set deal-breakers in relationships. Don't assume that someone knows how you feel no matter how long you have known that person. Don't think someone knows how you feel about a situation if you have not openly expressed it.

I've learned throughout the years that some people are scared to simply say "yes" or "no." You must learn to say yes and no and feel comfortable in doing so. Don't let anyone rob you of that choice.

In society, whether professional or personal relationships, I've learned that many of us are scared of the word "no" because we're scared of rejection. We do not like rejection. We're afraid of the way rejection makes us feel, and we're scared to tell other people "no" too. We will ignore emails and dodge conversations just to avoid saying "no." You might think that saying "no" will tarnish a relationship, friendship, or partnership, but "no" should be a part of everyone's vocabulary. Learning to say "yes" and "no" are things we were taught as kids. Those same words should be put to work in adulthood in all relationships, both personal and professional.

Throughout my career, and even in life, I had to build up the confidence to say "no" more and be prepared to deal with the consequences of when I said "yes." In life, we have choices. We have options. We get the privilege to decide, but we don't always get the privilege of choosing the consequences that are a direct reflection of those decisions.

Setting boundaries are good for all relationships. It helps define you and build character. What are your deal-breakers? Do you even know your own deal breakers, or do you fall for anything and accept what you are given? You must first understand who you are before you can accompany or complement anyone else.

What would end a relationship? What act would end a friendship or partnership? Write those deal breakers down and share them with your spouse, partner, or loved ones. You must understand what you can and cannot deal with. Even if you are not in a relationship, take this time to write down your deal breakers. Set respectful boundaries in your relationships and learn how to communicate them in a positive way.

Don't be afraid of rejection. Rejection can change your life for the better if you allow it.

If you do have a partner, take things a step further and right down your boundaries together so each party knows exactly what those deal breakers are, and there is no miscommunication later down the line.

Proper communication can prevent poor performance and deliverance. Learn to respectfully say "yes" and "no" in all relationships. Get as comfortable with saying "no," as you are in saying "yes." Also, don't be afraid of rejection. Rejection can change the direction of your life for the better if you allow it. It can not only make you stronger, but wiser. It can even make you work harder. All "no's" are not negatives.

Know your deal breakers in all relationships & communicate them.

PURE PEACE
AND
HARMONY
STARTS
WITHIN
YOU.

Turn from evil and
do good; seek peace
and pursue it.

— Psalm 34:14

CHAPTER 2

Take Care of Yourself
Don't Drain Your Well Trying to Fulfill Someone Else's

G od blessed me with the beautiful ability to love. I'm a nurturer, and I always strive to find the good in people, even when the bad outweighs the good. But I had to learn to love people from afar, even if it hurts. God wants us to be peacemakers and help others, but you must love yourself first before you can love someone else.

As the saying goes, you can't pour from an empty cup. You must have something to give to offer it to someone else. If you don't genuinely have love in your heart, how can you give it or receive it? If you don't have passion and compassion, how can you feel it for someone else? How can you support someone if you lack your own support system? If you aren't motivated, how can you motivate others? How can you share with someone a character trait you don't even possess?

Love is a powerful emotion, and it's meant to be shared. You can't keep love to yourself. Sometimes it may feel like a liability if you've encountered someone who abused or took advantage of your love, but it's really an asset and a gift. No matter how many times you've been hurt or deceived, you can't deny yourself of the ability to love. Throughout life, you may encounter individuals who will abuse the love you have in your heart and take advantage of your selfless emotions. But don't be ashamed of who you are. Don't let anyone belittle you because you choose to love and love unconditionally.

Many people love "conditionally" because that's the only type of love they've experienced. When they meet someone who loves them unconditionally, with no reservations, they cannot handle it or even understand it.

You were put on this earth to be extraordinary, not ordinary or typical, and that includes your relationships. It may take other extraordinary individuals to recognize just how extraordinary you are.

Those who are unable to see how extraordinary you are will question everything in your relationship because they're accustomed to conditional love. In their past failed relationships, the love changed when the conditions changed. That is not the type of relationship you want. Circumstances change daily, but your love shouldn't. You should never love a person based on conditions or solely on what a person can do for you.

> Don't be afraid to love no matter how many times you've been hurt.

Unconditional love has no limits. Unconditional love stays strong even through storms, struggles, and imperfect situations. If a person lost their job, money, or health, would you still love them?

I have also heard women and men use "unconditional love" as an excuse for staying in relationships that should have ended a long time ago. For example, I met a woman who had been cheated on multiple times, but she continued to stay in the relationship by saying she loved him unconditionally. Unconditional love shouldn't be an excuse for allowing someone to hurt you repeatedly. Unconditional love is not an excuse for unacceptable behavior. If that person can't respect the love you're giving, you must love yourself enough to recognize what's acceptable and unacceptable.

You are important, and your mental security should be a top priority. Self-care and mental maintenance is vital. Do you realize how important it is to take care of yourself? Some people may call this selfish but it's imperative. You must take care of yourself mentally, physically, and emotionally. You must fill your own well before someone else can drink from it. You must have love in your heart before someone else can feel it.

Have you ever forgiven a loved one, friend, colleague, or family member for hurting or disappointing you, and you continued in that relationship only to find out that it is emotionally and mentally draining you? I believe in second chances but don't let the same person keep hurting you or taking advantage of you. Don't drain your well trying to fulfill someone else's. Many people have drowned trying to save someone else. Don't break yourself trying to fix someone else.

Love shouldn't be draining. It isn't disrespectful, demanding, or jealous. Relationships, friendships, and even professional partnerships shouldn't consume so much of your energy that it starts to take you away from yourself.

We tend to do these things for people we love. But you must love yourself first. You should have so much love for yourself that it can't be compromised by someone else's choices or demands. You must love and respect yourself the same way you would want someone else to love and respect you.

People deal with hurt in different ways but no matter how many times you've been hurt, don't become someone you're not. When a relationship ends, the old cliché says that the fastest way to get over your ex-man or ex-woman is to get under a new one? But how many men and women do you want to get under? Don't cover up your pain with someone else. That's equivalent to not letting air get to a wound. You just want to cover it up with a Band-aid and never take it off to breathe. Don't compromise who you are in an effort to comfort yourself. You're worth more than that.

Ladies, we are all Queens. Protect your mind and protect your body. Your body is your temple. We have all made mistakes in the past we wish we could take back, but we can't. Mistakes don't define you. Even if you've been promiscuous in the past, you can move past that. Do not allow who you were or the things you've done interfere with who God wants you to ultimately become. Focus on who you are now and who you want to be. This starts with your lifestyle and your mindset. You can change your life just by changing your mind, and the way you think. When you start changing the way you think, you start changing the things you do.

Men, you are Kings who need Queens. Don't just pursue every big butt with a smile. When things don't go your way, or you feel a female has hurt you, stop sliding under the next one just to try to get over the previous one. Quit failing to acknowledge or deal with the pain or hurt of the previous relationship. Some of my best friends are guys and I know men can cover up hurt very well but moving from relationship to relationship could deflect deeper insecurities. Maybe you didn't have a mother to nurture you growing up, so you look for a woman to be your supporter and a means of emotional supply. Or maybe you had a mother who nurtured and catered to you too much growing up, and it has become an addiction for you to find that nurturing in every woman you meet.

I had a friend, a very strong and independent man, who shared with me before he passed that his lack of commitment but longing for companionship stemmed from the lack of relationship he had with his own mom. He was a good man but moved from relationship to relationship, whether he really liked a female or not. He was scared to be alone and had a problem with settling down with one woman for long periods of time. He believed that his issues stemmed from previous childhood trauma which he ultimately had to address and deal with as an adult.

I've been celibate a number of times throughout my adult life, even in long-term relationships. The fact that I practiced abstinence only ran away those men who it was supposed to run away rather quickly. Not everyone can accept it, and I had to respect that. But ladies, a man who is seriously interested in your well-being will accept you for who you are and respect your decision. There are men who are mature enough to embark on this journey with you. I do believe some men will wait for what they want. But it's not for the weak at heart or the weary. It's for the committed. It's for those who want to make a change in their life. It's for those who believe in change and want to embrace it. If someone genuinely embraces you, they will be receptive and will support you.

I dated a guy and gave him the book *The Wait* a couple of months after dating. I remember him reading it after weeks of holding on to it. We waited and never had sex. Ten months later, he proposed. We waited together. He entertained the journey I was on. I was traveling on a road to gain more insight on where I wanted to be and exploring the path that God had placed me on. He was a part of that journey. That's actually the point. You don't have to belittle yourself or compromise things you believe in just to be accepted or to be loved. The right man will love you just the way you are and exactly where you are.

People meet people at different points in their lives. I have learned throughout life that a person will do what he or she needs to do to get you in a position where they would like for you to be. Now once you are in that position, sometimes the rules change. It is up to you to stay in the game or gracefully decline not to play anymore.

Some people are scared of love; scared of opening themselves up for failure. Is it a risk? Absolutely. But isn't that what life is all about? We take risks on people all the time in business, relationships, and friendships. Marriage is the most extreme example. How many marriages have ended in divorce? Didn't that person take a risk on marrying the person they loved? How many friendships have ended because one person deceived another? How many times have you dated a person you had already heard was promiscuous, a liar, or a cheater? We all want to believe in relationships that a person would be different with us, and we strive to bring out the best in people, as we should. That should always be your goal.

How many of you have come across potential business partners who have failed at previous businesses but want to invest in a new one with you? Just because it failed with someone else doesn't mean it will necessarily fail with you. You can bring out the best in someone, just as you can bring out the worst. We take risks every day, whether big or small. We must know how to handle and take care of ourselves when taking those risks. This starts within us. Inner problems have inner solutions.

Can you handle the disappointment of a failed relationship or a failed business? Yes, you can. That's a part of life. That's a part of your story. That's a part of your growth.

In life, everything will not work out. Everything will not go your way. When problems or issues arise, a person's true character shows up. You've heard this before. When a person shows you who they really are, believe them.

Both men and women can be charming yet deceptive. Some of them have spent their whole lives perfecting the technique, both personally and professionally, so they've become pretty good at it. You may not be able to avoid those people, but you can control how you deal with them.

It's important to protect your energy. Sometimes it takes time to see people for who they really are. You may learn that you need to protect your energy from someone close to you: a loved one, friend, family member, or coworker. It can even be a parent. If you have someone in your life that continues to disrespect you and doesn't treat you the way you should be treated, you should accept that this is a toxic relationship and take steps to protect yourself from it. These relationships wreak havoc on your mind, body, and soul; stop allowing them to affect your energy. Stop giving life to it. You give life to the things you entertain and tolerate.

Recently at church, a young girl approached the alter asking for prayer for the friends and family of a middle school aged class-mate who had taken their own life. Our pastor, Pastor Jerry Young, reminded us that suicide is a permanent solution to a temporary problem. At such a young age, that person may not have been able to see past their current problems.

Even as adults, we are constantly presented with life-changing situations. Life doesn't come with a handbook, but it does come with supportive materials to help you through tough situations.

I've been blessed throughout life to have a great support system and I am thankful for it. This is important. Surround yourself with people who have your best interests at heart. Surround yourself with individuals who may not have the same goals as you, but they have goals. You may not be passionate about the same things but you both possess the same drive. Positive people usually bear positive results.

Peace of mind is more valuable than money itself. How many celebrities or rich entertainers have taken their own life or turned to drugs or alcohol and ended up in rehab? Don't equate money to happiness or peace of mind. Some things are priceless. Taking care of yourself mentally, physically, and emotionally are a few of those things. When you become healthier, you can become wealthier.

Have you ever asked yourself, "How are you doing?" Do you ever ask yourself, "How do you feel today?" Why? You ask others all the time. Why wouldn't you ask yourself? Just as you are concerned with others around you, you should be concerned about yourself. Take the time to analyze how you're really feeling. Mental exercise is important. Take care of yourself mentally and emotionally, and love yourself.

Throughout your life, ask yourself if the love you've received has been unconditional or conditional? How have those experiences impacted your relationships? How you have been loved affects how you love and your mentality.

When things don't work out the way we've planned,

> Do not allow who you were or the things you've done interfere with who God wants you to ultimately become.

sometimes we think it's the end of the world. But God doesn't always want us to be comfortable. Sometimes He wants us to be uncomfortable just because it helps develop our character. There are times when life is unfair and unjust, so we have to prepare ourselves for disappointment and even failure. However, failure isn't always a loss. Sometimes it's just a lesson. The way you handle situations that don't go your way shows who you really are.

When things don't go as you planned in the time you planned them, how do you handle it? How do you handle rejection or unexpected delays? Answer these questions in the space below and ask yourself how you can do better at handling things that don't go your way? How do you handle life's unexpected curveballs?

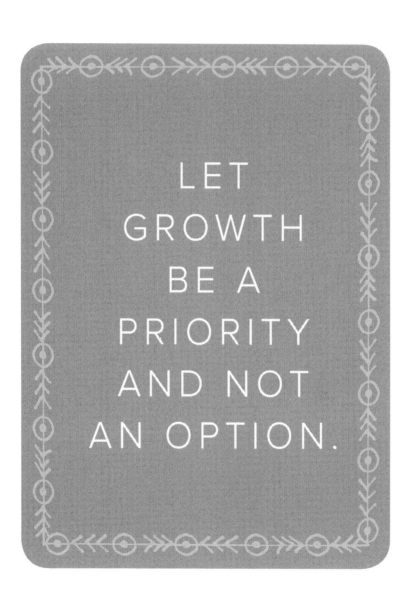

LET
GROWTH
BE A
PRIORITY
AND NOT
AN OPTION.

People will be
lovers of themselves,
lovers of money, boastful, proud,
abusive, disobedient to their parents,
ungrateful, unholy, without love,
unforgiving, slanderous, without
self-control, brutal, not lovers of the good,
treacherous, rash, conceited, lovers of
pleasure rather than lovers of God—
having a form of godliness but denying
its power. Have nothing to do
with them.

— 2 Timothy 3:2

CHAPTER 3

Discover New Boundaries

A few years ago, I did a casting interview for a television show. One of the questions they asked me was, "What was one of the craziest moments in your life when it came to relationships?"

Well, there was a guy, a very good professional athlete. He was tall, handsome, kind, knowledgeable, very attentive, and single. One day he asked me to meet him at a local restaurant to discuss a business deal he had been contemplating. But there was a big catch to this meeting. I certainly didn't see it coming.

It turned out that his "business deal" was a proposition. He wanted to pay me a million dollars to have his child. That was one of the things he felt like he was missing in his life. I would receive a house and a monthly stipend in addition to the million dollars. Our child would live in the best neighborhoods and attend the best schools. Since we weren't in a relationship and had never even been intimate, he knew I wouldn't hassle him and the child would be raised within a great family.

I was in disbelief. I had seen and heard a lot of things throughout my life but this one was unbelievable. Many ladies would take this offer, right? I know women who have sex for free every day and get pregnant without anything close to what this man was offering. He wanted to have his attorneys draw up the contracts to make this business deal official. Let's keep in mind this man was worth a few million dollars, and this offer would not have put a significant dent in his bank account. As a matter of fact, he had just secured another lucrative contract. All I had to do was say, "yes," but I was still sitting there with my mouth wide open in shock.

I've learned over the years many people will go to the extreme to obtain the things they want in life, even if that means buying it. But are you for sale? I've heard the saying everything can be bought and everything has a price. That may true, but the rest of my life wasn't for sale that day.

Did I think about his offer? Of course! No one had ever offered me a million dollars in my life to do anything! I tossed and turned all night. I couldn't even sleep. But I kept hearing God speak to me. "Now you know this is wrong Tambra, and the mere fact you are entertaining this thought in your head isn't right," He told me.

I created all kind of scenarios in my head to try to justify it. I could be financially stable and have a child to love and adore at the same time. But the morals and values that had been deeply instilled within me growing up wouldn't allow me to seriously entertain his offer. It's those little voices we hear that keep us grounded to who we really are and show us the correct choice.

If you don't stand for something, you will fall for anything. Know who you are and what you stand for. Set boundaries. In life, you will discover new boundaries. This proposition had been brought to me with such respect and kind words, I almost forgot what exactly he was asking of me.

This goes back to preparation. I was prepared to say no. I was groomed to say no. My maturity level allowed me to say no. I was prepared for this conversation and didn't even know it.

All those years of going to church and practicing my faith helped guide me in the right direction. Choosing to decline this offer was a turning point in my personal life. I'm not saying I haven't sinned because Lord knows I truly have, but this was a new level I had never been introduced to before. I realized then how much I had matured and grown. I am confident I made the right choice. I was forced to set new boundaries.

Don't let anyone make you feel bad for who you are and what you believe in. I believe in honesty and having open communication in all relationships. I believe in being kind to those who are kind to you, and even to those who are not.

Have you ever walked in a room and said, "Good Morning," and no one said a word back? I have, and I just said it again louder and with more energy! That's just a part of who I am. However, I have learned over time sometimes being too nice, lending a helping hand, and having a good heart can backfire. Some people take your kindness for weakness or attempt to run over you altogether.

That's unfortunate for me, because all my life I was taught to do right by others. However, don't feel bad for being kind. Don't feel bad for having a good heart. We all make some unfortunate decisions in our lives but when you are genuine, and you genuinely do things out of the kindness of your heart, you can't feel bad. Too often we apologize for having a helping hand and heart. But aren't we supposed to help others? Some of us have a helping heart and a nurturing soul. It's hard to turn that off.

> Don't let anyone make you feel bad for who you are & what you believe in.

My kindness has been taken for weakness several times throughout my life. People who said they would never hurt me still betrayed me. So you might ask, "Why are you still so kind? Why are you still so forgiving?" Those character qualities are just a part of who I am, and I was always willing to take that risk.

Has anyone ever told you that you're too nice or too loyal? I had a friend steal from me, but I forgave her, and to this day I've always been nice to her. That's maturity. If she needed me, I would still be there for her. I've had females who I thought were "friends" lie to me and lie about me. I've had men cheat, lie to my face, and I still forgave them. I pray for people who I know have stopped praying for me. Who does that? A child of God. How can you do that? Growth. Maturity.

Throughout the years, you work to become the person you want to grow to be. You get better. Thoughts of fear, discouragement, unforgiveness, resentment, hate, and retaliation are all works of the devil. You can't allow those thoughts to linger in your mind or co-exist in your heart. When you're a child of God, those thoughts become filled with faith, drive, understanding, encouragement, and confidence. Love lives in your heart. It easy to love when you have love in your heart and it's easier to do right, when you know what's right.

Social media is very popular, and I often see people post encouraging messages and scriptures on their social media pages. Well you can't post scriptures and encouraging messages all day if you're not applying them to your everyday life in some way. You can't believe in the Word and not try to walk in it at all.

For example, I saw a young lady post on social media about forgiveness and her love for the Lord. Later that same day, she posted venting about a friend request she had received on Facebook from a young lady she went to high school with. She posted, "Why would you send me a friend request when we didn't even like each other in high school?" Many years had obviously passed, and this attitude was the exact opposite of the scriptures and encouraging messages she had been posting. Become better, not bitter.

It's hypocritical to preach the Word and spread the Word if you're not actively trying to practice it daily yourself. You can't encourage forgiveness, peace and unity if you fail to forgive and communicate within your own relationships.

You want to motivate others, but you lack motivation and drown in self-pity. You want to encourage and talk about growth, but you fail to grow yourself in many areas of your own life. You want to point the finger at someone else and recognize all their faults, and what they did wrong, but you fail to recognize or acknowledge your own. You want to encourage maturity, but you lack that same quality when dealing with your own family and friends. You go to church to hear the Word and occupy a seat, but you fail to incorporate the message.

Stop being hearers of the message and start being doers. We've all struggled with this. Stop paraphrasing motivational messages and start taking heed to those messages, and act upon them yourself before encouraging others to do so. Everyone wants to talk about growth, but not everyone wants to put in the work that it takes to grow. If you really want to grow and become a better version of yourself, you have to analyze your life and make changes where appropriate. You can't expect to get different results if you continue doing the same things.

Do you really want to grow? Do you really want to be a better version of you? How do you handle conflict? When a relationship or friendship doesn't go your way, how do you deal with it? Do you turn to violence? Do you become cold and distant? Do you become bitter? Do you shut down communication or turn to verbal abuse? I can tell how far one has grown by simple actions and responses when things don't go their way. If you're doing any of these things, it's not a sign of growth or maturity.

Growth and maturity means accepting your faults and wrong-doings, owning up to them and apologizing to anyone you may have hurt in the process. Growth and maturity is learning to effectively communicate with others no matter what problems prevail. Growth is taking the initiative to ask for forgiveness when you know you have done wrong. Growth is admitting the truth when you know you have lied. Growth is helping someone who has undeniably hurt you. Growth is taking responsibility for your actions; actively practicing the things you encourage others to do. Growth is respectively doing what's right when you have a history of doing what's wrong.

I see a lot of women today promoting female empowerment and I applaud those who are genuinely non-biased and want to see other women win in their professional and personal endeavors. I value their creativity to bring us together and stand united. I've worked with some amazing women empowerment organizations and I thank each one of them for including me as a part of their vision. The women I have worked with in this capacity have all been authentic, ambitious, and dedicated to their purpose.

But I will be honest. On the other hand, I've also seen some women who stand behind a platform of female empowerment, but behind closed doors they have nothing but negative things to say about their female counterparts. You can't empower women and at the same time entertain the gossip and rumors about them in private conversations. You can't empower another woman if you're jealous of her. You can't pick and choose which women you want to empower.

There is already enough division and chaos going on in the world. You can't be one of the individuals who promote unity and love amongst each other, but ultimately lack it themselves. You must start with yourself first. You have to start with your own relationships. Trying to dim someone else's light is not going to make yours shine any brighter any sooner.

Ask yourself who you are and what do you stand for? Have you recently discovered new boundaries? Write them down.

_____

_____

_____

_____

_____

_____

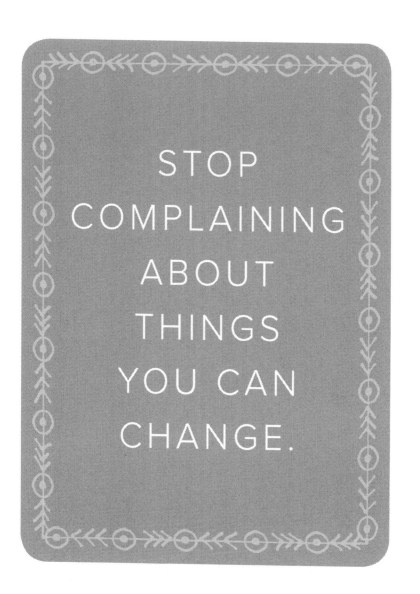

STOP
COMPLAINING
ABOUT
THINGS
YOU CAN
CHANGE.

Be kind and
compassionate to one
another, forgiving each
other, just as in Christ God
forgave you.

— Ephesians 4:32

CHAPTER 4

Practice Forgiveness
Forgive Others and Definitely Forgive Yourself

I learned very early in life that people will hurt you and disappoint you. Everyone does not share the same morals, standards, values, and beliefs. Everyone does not have the same heart as you. You must accept that people will hurt you even when you think they will not, or they have promised not to.

People make promises they will not keep. People make commitments they will break. This was one of the hardest lessons I had to learn. I always strive to keep my word throughout my life, so I had a hard time understanding why I was not receiving the same in return. I had even kept my word to those who knowingly hurt me, disappointed me, betrayed me, and even stole from me. It took some failed relationships and friendships to help realize that it wasn't me. Some people are raised differently.

Not everyone is raised out of love and compassion for other people. Sometimes people are left to raise themselves and they're fighting to just survive their childhood. Love, honesty, and loyalty are words they are just not use to hearing. Many men and women do not know what loyalty is. Loyal is an adjective. Loyalty is a characteristic. It can't be turned on and off. Either you have it or you don't.

Many people don't fully have the capability to understand what it means to be dedicated, faithful and truthful. They cannot fully understand that keeping your word can take you places and open doors of opportunities for you because of the promises you have vowed to keep.

How many of us have heard broken promises in relationships, friendships, and even in business? I used to consider myself a pretty good judge of character until I realized that I was basing my opinion on a persona that was only a façade. The characteristics they exhibited were meant to overshadow and conceal the realities of their true deeper emotional selves.

The things we experience growing up can affect who we become as adults. Growing up, I was surrounded by love and gratefulness. I took nothing for granted. I was appreciative. My family and I prayed over everything. I watched my parents work hard and go to work every day while raising two daughters with two very different personalities. As a child, I never saw my parents fight. I'm sure they had disagreements, but they never did it in front of my sister and I.

I also spent a lot of time with my grandparents, and I don't recall ever seeing them have a disagreement. All I saw was the love, admiration, and appreciation they had for one another. I admired their union. My grandfather adored my grandmother until the moment he took his very last breath, where she was right there by his side. At a very young age, their union showed me the meaning of true love. I saw how a man could adore you, love you, and appreciate you daily. I saw how a man valued the woman he loved. I saw love firsthand early on. Not only in one relationship, but in two.

My parents and grandparents were great examples of true love and commitment. So, growing up, I never saw a man and a woman who love each other argue and fight. But as I got older, I started developing friendships with people who had. I would meet a boy who was raised by a single mother and his father walked out of his life in his teens. I'd meet a girl whose father was completely absent from her life and all she knows is her mother. I'd meet a boy whose grandparents raised him, and he never knew his parents at all. I'd meet a girl whose parents divorced at an early age, and all she saw growing up were arguments and fights. I'd meet a boy whose parents were together, but all he saw was cheating and the back and forth of working it out.

Could this affect the way a person loves? Do these things we see early in life affect the way we interact with others, and determine how close we will allow individuals to get to us? Absolutely. You can develop trust issues early on just from watching others use and misuse loved ones. However, you don't have to be shaped by your environment. You can change. Like Jay Z said, "You can't heal what you never reveal." You must reveal the problem first before making an attempt to heal it. A person must learn the root of why they are the way they are. Issues must be addressed before problems can be put to rest. You can't learn the lesson if you don't admit there is a problem. Just like it's hard to learn from a mistake that you never really even acknowledge making. Growth is a necessity we all need but you must want to grow.

If you want to be forgiven of anything in your life, you must practice forgiveness first.

Men and women are very good at masking. I've watched men put on mask after mask to get what they want from the woman they desire. But the thing about masks, they must come off at some point. You will eventually get tired of hiding behind it. Someone will do something that will force you to angrily throw your mask off and reveal the person you really are.

People tend to guard their hearts, their minds, and their feelings because of things they saw in previous relationships, even if those relationships weren't theirs. They had an early impact upon their life. Things we constantly see and are around can impact our lives in ways we don't see or realize until later. However, even if you were abused or misused as a child, that doesn't give you the right to abuse and misuse others.

When people hurt or disappoint me, I use to shut down communication, so I wouldn't say things that I would regret later. I needed space to think and process the situation. That was my version of controlling my tongue. It wasn't until someone later helped me realize the importance of communicating with those you care about, although it was hard for them to do it themselves. I realized as I matured, my thoughts and behavior changed as I was on a path to spiritual and personal growth. I had to learn how to deal with things and people in a more mature way. I learned through scripture that it was a sin to turn your back on someone who needs you.

People will disappoint you. That's just a fact of life, and it's up to you to decide how to deal with it. You cannot let others have so much control over your life that it affects your happiness and well-being. When people disappoint or hurt you, pray about it, forgive them, and move forward. Give it to God.

Practice having a heart of forgiveness. Some people will ask why you choose to forgive someone who has wronged you. Do not allow people to manipulate you into feeling guilty because you have a good, forgiving heart. Notice that I am saying forgiveness and not passiveness. Forgiveness is for you. Forgiveness affects how you live and how you go about your daily activities. It affects your mind and your soul.

Growing up in church, as kids we were taught about forgiveness. If someone sins against you, rebuke the sin, not the person. If they repent, forgive them. But what if they don't openly repent? What if that person who hurt you or mistreated you doesn't apologize? Can you forgive them? The answer should be yes. There is poison in not forgiving. Not having a forgiving heart poisons your mind and body. Why would you want to do harm to yourself at the fault of someone else? Overcome the obstacle that was meant to hurt you and allow it to better you.

As a radio personality, I often interact with music executives and various promoters on events. A few years ago, I was contacted about hosting a Hip-Hop concert by an out-of-town promoter. I agreed. I was traveling in Miami when he called and told me his vision. I initially thought it was short notice for such a concert, but I wasn't asked for my opinion on the logistics. I was only being contacted as a talent.

The promoter had a good history of doing business with the radio station and once again, I thought I considered myself a pretty good judge of character. Later I learned I would be hosting with actress Vivica A. Fox. I agreed, and we negotiated on a price. I remember drawing up the contract. He came by the radio station and prepaid for commercials, but I didn't require upfront payment. That was a bad decision on my part. He promised to pay me on the day of the event.

The concert went on as planned and I had a great time hosting with the talented actress. However, at the end of the night, the promoter didn't pay me as agreed. He said he would come by the station on Monday and pay me. Needless to say, I still haven't been paid despite numerous promises. I was patient and compassionate as the promoter offered me endless excuses.

Hopefully my lesson will be a blessing to someone else. Ultimately, I realized I had to move past that situation and forgive the promoter for never paying me for a job that I did. I also had to forgive myself for putting too much faith in him by not getting my deposit upfront.

This goes back to saying that some people will disappoint you no matter how much faith you have in a person. Of course, it hurts more in relationships because your heart is involved.

Who are some people who have hurt you, betrayed you, or gone back on their word? Write those names down and practice saying you forgive them. Do it for yourself. If you want to be forgiven of anything in your life, you must practice forgiveness first.

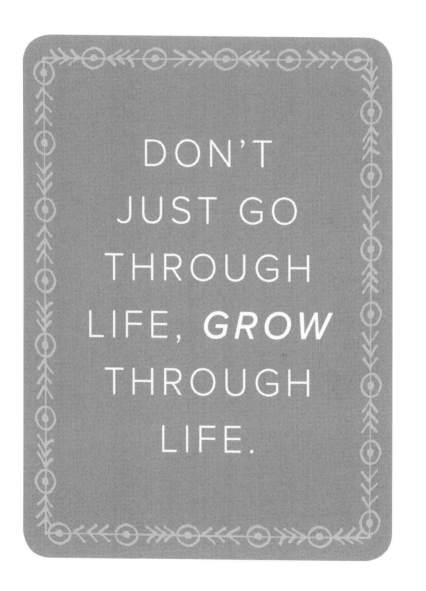

DON'T JUST GO THROUGH LIFE, *GROW* THROUGH LIFE.

The Lord is my rock,
my fortress and my deliverer;
my God is my rock, in whom I
take refuge. He is my shield and
the horn of my salvation, my
stronghold. I call to the Lord, who is
worthy of praise, and I am saved
from my enemies.

— Psalm 18: 2-3

CHAPTER 5

Have Faith That God Protects You Despite the Circumstances

I recently met a woman, a nurse, who had been married for several years, and she shared her story with me. She and her husband had two children together. One day, he left for work and never came back. She later learned that he had left her for another woman, who happened to be his cousin.

This woman was so embarrassed about her situation that she had stopped going to church. She didn't know how to face other people who were used to seeing her there with her husband. She only went to work and home. Even though she was having a difficult time, this young lady still had a beautiful smile and a very bubbly personality. I wouldn't have known about her situation if she hadn't shared it with me.

To paraphrase a sermon by Bishop T.D. Jakes, when people walk out of your life, you have to let them walk. Your future is not tied to someone who voluntarily leaves you. I used to have a hard time understanding how a person can claim to love someone yet turn around and hurt that person so badly, especially after building a life together. But you cannot force someone to be somewhere they do not want to be.

Learn to master your emotions. Use what was meant to hurt you to empower you.

She was hurt when he left, and she had plenty of emotional bumps and bruises. But I could see that her situation didn't break her. His quiet departure may have been the best thing for her and her family. When people walk out of your life, it's for your own protection. It's God way of keeping you safe and preparing you for the next chapter. No one likes rejection, but it's a part of life, and its important because it forces you to grow.

Throughout the years, I have met many couples and ladies who have shared their stories of hurt, deceit, and betrayal. I've met a woman who spent fourteen years of her life with a man until one day he puts his hands on her in front of her child. We all would like to think that we know a person after spending fourteen years with them, but do we really? Do you ever really know your spouse?

Is there a time frame for how long you should date before you get married? Its seems to be different for everyone. I've seen couples fall in love, get engaged eight months later, and they are still together until this day. I've seen other couples who've fallen in love, gotten married, and saw another side of their spouse years later. They're now divorced.

People can grow and change, but they can also change for the worst. We all want a fairy tale love story, but does it really exist? Every woman wants to be treated like a Queen and every man wants to be treated like a King, but don't be so blinded by the honeymoon phase in the beginning that you fail to pay attention to possible red flags.

As I spoke more in detail with the nurse whose husband had left her, it became clear that she had ignored warning signs early in the relationship. He was once a charming man, but later turned mean, manipulative, and mentally abusive. She said his attitude and demeanor changed often. She justified it because the good outweighed the bad, and they had children together. She tried to do everything as a woman to keep the marriage together, but he had already checked out.

As women, we are more prone to working things out for the better. That day, she reminded me that she remembered her vows. For better or worse. That same man that took vows and once treated her the best had now treated her the worst.

How can you hurt someone you genuinely love? How can you openly mistreat someone you care about? How can you down talk or verbally abuse someone you're in love with? I later learned through other women the meaning of the word narcissist. I was introduced to narcissistic characteristics and sociopath personality traits. That's how the woman's husband could easily walk away from an entire family with no remorse. It was a personality disorder and an immoral disconnection.

He walked away and never looked back. He didn't just walk out of her life, but their children's lives as well, leaving them with emotional scars. But I still believe that him leaving was ultimately the best thing for her and her family. There are some things in life we may not understand, but we must believe that God knows what's best for His children.

Even if a person isn't physically abusive, verbal abuse is very real in a relationship. The tongue is a powerful tool. It can be used for good and it can also be used for evil. It can build relationships and it can also single handedly destroy them. Words can hurt, especially coming from someone you love.

Verbal abuse is not to be taken lightly. Mothers have hurt daughters with their words. Fathers have hurt sons. Parents have hurt their children with words that will stick with them throughout their entire lives. Lovers have hurt spouses with their words. Words have ruined relationships, hurt friendships, and divided families. Relationships that could have been mended have been destroyed by words. However, when someone hurts you with words, no matter how much it hurts, you have to learn not to retaliate with hurt. Especially, if you are on a path towards becoming a better person.

I know men and women who have been verbally abused throughout their life who became verbally abusive themselves as a defense mechanism. Hurt people hurt people. Remember, you must be careful of what you entertain and give life to. You can unknowingly start to put out what you start taking in. Negativity can attract negativity in its responses no matter how positive you try to be. Don't let a hurt man or woman change who you are.

The scripture teaches us to be slow to anger. But how can you be positive when someone you love can be so negative towards you? I believe in the power of prayer and the power of maturity. Most people have been hurt before by someone with their words or their actions. I will admit I was the type of female who had never been in any type of abusive relationship before, and I had never even had a man to say a bad word to me in any relationship nor in my friendships. That was foreign to me. To be disrespected by a man was unknown to me and I wish that disrespect upon no one.

How you deal with displeasure and get over disappointment determines who you are. Your true character is tested in times of distress, disappointment, and hurt. Your integrity is tested. Your self-control is tested. Your spirit is tested. Your faith is even tested. Your mind is tested.

I learned through scripture that you are not a master of self-control if you cannot control what you say or what you do in times of emotional stress. However, James 2:26 teaches us that if anyone considers himself religious and yet does not keep a tight rein on his tongue, he deceives himself and his religion is worthless. Is your religion worthless?

Sometimes we find purpose in our pain and clarity in our confusion. Can you be the bigger person when someone hurts you? We all have made mistakes in life and had moments we wish we could get back, so we could do things differently or react in another way. But the truth of the matter is that we can't repeat the past. We can only accept our mistakes, apologize if we hurt anyone in the process, and move forward to being a better person in the future.

Everyone deals with hurt and anger differently. If you are a spiritual being, I advise you to rest your soul on a higher being. Shift your focus. Believe in the power of prayer and the power of forgiveness. I struggled with forgiveness growing up for a long time, but I had to realize that no one should have that much power over your emotions.

I've always tried to practice honesty in relationships, friendships and business, but I later realized some people cannot handle the truth. I still encourage couples to practice honesty in relationships. Dishonesty kills relationships. It's sad, but some people just don't have the truth in them. They have been lying so much throughout their lives that they've come to believe their own lies. Covering up the truth can kill a relationship just as much as a bold lie. Relationships built on lies, deception, and manipulation will not last.

Has someone recently hurt you, or is there someone you've hurt? Did you apologize? Did you acknowledge the fact that you were hurt so you can begin to heal? Has someone deceived you or lied to you? Write that person's name down and recognize the pain so you can begin to heal.

All wounds heal if they are nursed properly. You must take care of yourself. I want you to learn how to master your emotions and not let anyone or anything negatively affect your daily routine, attitude or behavior. What you focus on grows. What you give your attention to intensifies.

Imagine focusing on yourself and giving yourself the attention you may tend to give others. Healing is a part of your growth. Focus on yourself, your growth, and your healing. Use what was meant to hurt you to empower you.

LEARN
TO STAY
WITHIN
PEACE.

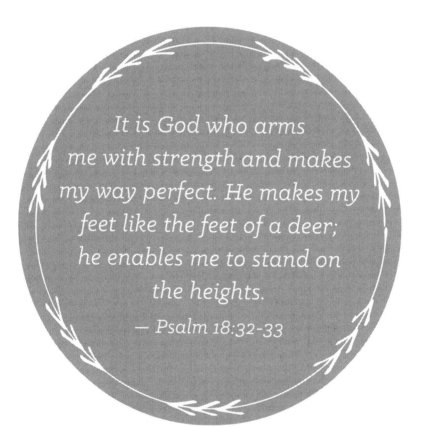

*It is God who arms
me with strength and makes
my way perfect. He makes my
feet like the feet of a deer;
he enables me to stand on
the heights.*

— Psalm 18:32-33

CHAPTER 6

Don't Treat Others How You Were Mistreated
Be Better Than Them

It's easier to forgive someone if they recognize their faults and apologize, but not everyone is going to do that. Throughout my life, I was always taught to apologize and ask for forgiveness if I made a mistake or hurt someone's feelings. But everyone wasn't taught that. How do you handle being hurt by someone insensitive?

Friends and family may give you different advice on how to handle these types of situations. Some will tell you to get mad, while others will tell you to study the Bible and seek answers in prayer. There is no "right" way to deal with insensitive or apathetic individuals. You must do what feels right for you. Retaliation or getting upset is a waste of energy. You can put that energy towards something greater that will benefit you in a more positive way. Don't be one of those hurt people that hurts other people.

That's why you must be careful of the things and people you entertain. Things you take in can easily become things you start to put out. You cannot go throughout your life hurting other people, just because you've been hurt by a loved one, a friend, a family member or even a parent.

I grew up in the church and attended a Baptist pre-school. Ever since I was born, I've been taught to love and have love in your heart for others. Some of us consider love and compassion for complete strangers a weakness, but it takes strength to love. I mentioned the risks we take in love in the previous chapters: the risk of being hurt, disappointed, or deceived. You have to decide if it's worth the risk.

I still remember getting my heart broken for the first time. It's a feeling I thought I would never forget (at that moment). I thank God for His protection throughout the idiotic decision I made many years ago.

When I was a teenager in high school, my boyfriend graduated first and went on to college. Since I was still in high school, he came back home on the weekends to visit. One sunny Saturday, we were at his parents' house laughing and talking outside as usual. Well evidently, he hadn't paid attention to his car. His car was dirty, and I noticed that someone had written, "I love you and will miss you," on it.

Obviously, I asked about it, and he came up with some lie to shut me up. We argued about it and I left. Once he made it back to school, he admitted that a girl he was seeing in college had written the message on his car and he didn't know how to tell me. I was furious that he had lied to my face.

I remember hanging up on him and calling back later, but he stopped answering the phone. Today's Tambra Cherie, much more mature, would just go to sleep and go about my business. But the fifteen-year-old Tambra was blinded by hurt and deceit. I snuck out of the house with my father's gun and drove more than two hours to my boyfriend's college in the middle of the night. I called him from the phone in the lobby of his dorm and told him I needed to talk to him.

We met downstairs and talked in the car. He was shocked and concerned that I had driven so far by myself. I was in tears. He tried to comfort me but was still distant – maybe because of the pistol resting next to me on the seat. The pistol had no bullets in it; it was just there. Maybe it was a scare tactic to let him know how hurt I was. After our talk, my emotions were all over the place. I called my parents, who had no idea I had even left. They thought I was asleep. My parents, and my sister drove over two hours to come get me in the middle of the night.

My father drove my car back home, and I promise that was the longest two hours ever. He was disappointed in my behavior, but he also understood that I was hurt. He advised me that I needed to make better decisions. I think I was more hurt than anything by seeing the hurt in his face. I share this story with you just to show that many of us have experienced hurt and deceit.

Later, when I was in college, about nineteen years old, I went out one night with my best friend. We both used fake IDs to get into a club. While we were getting drinks, my boyfriend at the time called. I walked to the restroom, so I could hear over the loud music. He told me that it was late, and he was going to bed. I went back in the club to party with my friend, but something didn't feel right. I've always taken my time to process information even after we've had a full discussion. My intuition kicked in and I told my friend about the conversation. One of us said, "Let's go!" Without any hesitation, we got in the car and drove straight to his house. Just as I suspected, his car wasn't there. I knocked on the door, already knowing he wasn't home. However, I knew that before I even made it there.

In this situation, I knew he had lied to me. I could have easily gone home. But I didn't; I was furious. So instead of going home, we drove by his best friend's house nearby. As we pulled into the parking lot, I could see his car parked in front of his best friend's apartment. As I got out of the car, he met me coming down the stairs. "Weren't you supposed to be asleep?" I asked him. He immediately started getting defensive and told my best friend to take me home. I wasn't listening to anything he was saying. All I could think about was the fact that he came outside to meet me at the bottom of the steps. I ran up the stairs before he could stop me and opened the door to the apartment. Inside was his best friend watching a movie with a young lady, and his ex-girlfriend, who was sitting by herself, obviously waiting for him to come back inside. I remember hollering to the room, "Oh we're watching movies!? Its movie night!?"

I left all of them behind that night. I share these stories to show that we've all been hurt and lied to, whether we know it or not. We've all made bad decisions in life. We've been hurt by people we love and care about. However, I also shared to show that you get over it. Time goes on, and you move beyond it. As you can see, it becomes a part of your story. I look back and laugh at these encounters and thank God for growth!

I've heard and seen a lot throughout the years. That's why I talk about relationships a lot. I've created bonds with many of my listeners over the years just from talking about relationships. Ladies, we all have stories. You might meet a charming gentleman who treats you like a queen. He makes promises and vows to love you for life, through all the good times and hard times. But, years later, even in marriage, the man you met is no longer the man you fell in love with. He changes. In some cases, you don't even recognize him anymore. He changes the way he acts toward you. This can come at no fault of your own.

Don't allow anyone to manipulate you into thinking their wrongdoings are a direct reflection of something you've done or said. Whatever action taken was a choice they made. Their actions are their decisions. I've heard women try to blame themselves when their spouse cheats on them or has a wandering eye. I've also heard men give countless excuses for the reasons they've cheated or changed. No matter what your situation may be, no one deserves to be hurt or deceived by someone they love. No one deserves physical, emotional or verbal abuse. It is unacceptable in all relationships.

I don't want to leave out the men, because it may have happened to you too. You might meet a woman who you believe loves you for who you are. Later, you find out that she cheated on you, lied, or only wanted to be with you because of the things you could offer her financially. There are some women who only want to be taken care of by men and want to accept the role of a housewife while her man works to provide. Sometimes these women even look like go-getters, only waiting for the right bait to stop going to get it. They put on all the charm in the world and make you feel like you are the center of theirs. They may not genuinely love you, but they love the lifestyle you can provide. Deception hurts. You should never intentionally deceive someone to achieve a goal.

God doesn't promise to eliminate life's challenges. He promises to give you the strength to overcome those challenges and frustrations. Do you feel like someone has intentionally deceived you? Have you intentionally deceived someone? Make it right today. It's never too late to right your wrongs.

> Be careful of the things & people you entertain.

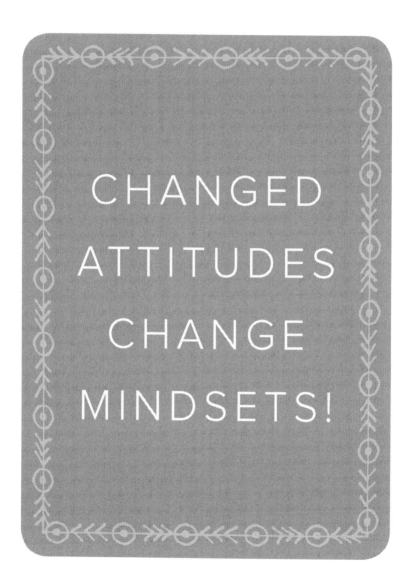

CHANGED
ATTITUDES
CHANGE
MINDSETS!

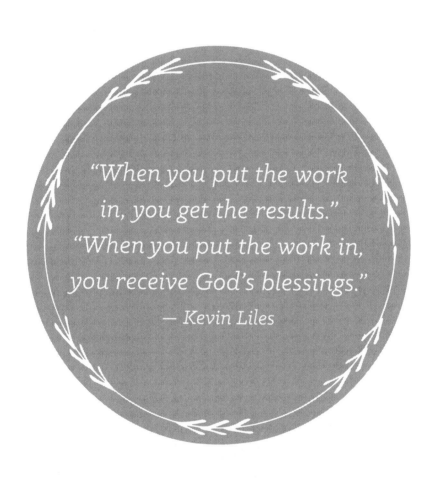

"When you put the work in, you get the results." "When you put the work in, you receive God's blessings."

— Kevin Liles

CHAPTER 7

Don't Be Afraid of Change

We are responsible for ourselves and we can only change ourselves. You can't change someone who doesn't want to change. No matter how much you want to see a person grow, mature, and succeed, that person must want to do it for themselves. We all get older, but everyone doesn't mature at the same pace, and some people don't want to mature at all. Just as you don't possess the power to change people, you also don't have the power to change their mindset. These things come with growth, love and maturity.

Love should be genuine. For a person who has only experienced conditional love throughout their lives, that may be the only type of love they're able to give. People only loved them with conditions, when it was convenient or when they could do something for them. Stay away from this type of love; it's only a waste of time and energy.

I admire ex-couples who have remained friends and are still able to respect each other even after their intimate relationship has ended. I knew one couple that had been married for years and had children together. Due to infidelity, a child was born outside the marriage. This led them to divorce, but they were still able to respect each other and co-parent. They remained friends in moving forward in their other relationships. They didn't bash each other or disrespect each other.

Often, a person's true character doesn't reveal itself until the relationship or friendship has run its course. The way a person treats you after the relationship has ended shows a lot about who they really are.

When you initially meet someone, you're meeting his or her representative. People can only hide behind the persona for so long. Of course, you want to put your best foot forward upon initially meeting someone, but that persona should be a true representation of who you really are. Unfortunately, it doesn't always work out that way in reality.

Nowadays, a person's true character may not be revealed until months or years later. Be cautious in dealing with individuals whose emotions and feelings are constantly changing. Genuine love doesn't change just because a person hurt you or did something you dislike. People often question why individuals stay in a relationship with a cheating spouse. The answer is not complicated. Sometimes love makes you do things you wouldn't necessarily do. When you genuinely love someone, you fight for him or her. You fight for relationships you want. If you genuinely love someone, you don't stop loving them overnight because he or she cheated.

Let me share a story that may not sound like the typical love story. It involves dishonesty, but it also involves truth and patience. It involves work, dedication, and forgiveness.

Understand you can only change yourself & your OWN attitude.

A boy and girl met when they were very young and dated for years. They were high school sweethearts. As college approached, these two lovebirds grew even closer. But college brought new temptations. Both men and women can be tempted, but it's up to us to stay strong in the face of temptation if we're in committed relationships. In this love story, the man fell for temptation. Even though the young man loved his girlfriend, he cheated.

Even though you love the Lord, you still sin. No one is perfect. Now please understand, I am not saying that cheating is acceptable under any circumstances. It is wrong and can destroy a relationship that took years to build. Trust takes years to develop and can be destroyed in an instant. It takes a sincere, committed effort to get it back once destroyed.

However, in this love story, the woman forgave her high school sweetheart for being unfaithful. They went through a very rough patch, but there are trials in every relationship. When there's genuine love, it's hard to give up on the relationship. It's up to you to decide if the relationship is worth fighting for and if the person is worth the fight.

These two high school sweethearts eventually got married, had children, and are still married more than forty years later. So, in this love story, it was worth the fight. They got their happy ending.

Every good love story starts with a beautiful beginning and concludes with a happy ending, but sometimes we don't hear about the part in the middle. If they had not weathered the storm over 40 years ago, they wouldn't have their beautiful children and grandchildren today.

A couple of years ago, I had the pleasure of interviewing Hip Hop music executive Kevin Liles, a veteran in the business. One thing he said really stuck with me. "When you put the work in, you get the results," he said. "But you have to put in the work. When you put the work in, you receive God's blessings."

You have to put in the work to get the results you want to achieve, whether in business, school, or life in general. This is true for relationships as well, as long as both parties are willing to put in the work equally. If it were too easy and too accessible, would you really want that?

WANT TO GROW? LET IT GO.

I cannot walk in
my future with my
foot in my past.

— Tommie Mabry

CHAPTER 8

Quit Living in the Past

You may have truly loved someone who hurt you, or there may be a friend or family member who turned their back on you when you needed them the most. You may have even had a parent or sibling maliciously abuse you growing up. Maybe a significant other cheated on you, even after they promised they would never hurt you. You may have found a relationship that you thought was everything you'd prayed for, only to have it end badly. Your loved one may have broken vows that you both promised to keep. It may have left you feeling confused and hurt, wondering how the person who promised to always have your back is no longer around. You're left with good memories as well as bad ones and they're playing over and over in your mind. You may even be ashamed of things you've done in the past and you constantly beat yourself up about it. It's time to let it go.

Never underestimate any chapter in your life. Every chapter happened for a reason. It prepared you for what's coming next. Through hurt, there is healing. You are being made.

There have been times in my life when I've been cheated on, deceived, verbally abused, taken advantage of, or manipulated. I've been hurt by people I've loved and trusted. I've been a victim of crimes. But I didn't let those experiences break me or define me. Overcoming those obstacles helped mold me.

I've made mistakes and decisions that I use to wish I could take back. I later realized those mistakes and decisions helped make me who I am today no matter how much turmoil or stress it may have caused. God has always protected me. No matter what you're going through, never let a situation kill your spirit or faith. You know who you are, and you know your worth. Every test is testimony. Quit giving energy and life to things that don't deserve a second thought. It doesn't even deserve your attention.

I've seen and heard so much throughout the years. I've had conversations with people who dread going to work because of cruel co-workers. That same coworker who makes their job miserable might be the same person we see in church every Sunday. I often wondered how some people who go to church every week and read the scriptures can be very angry and dishonest in a different environment. I didn't know how that was possible until a sermon was shared with me about "second hand faith." It's possible for someone to attend church faithfully and hear the sermons, but if it isn't their own faith, they cannot fully understand the message and act upon it.

Many people have been taught to go to church because it's the "right" thing to do, but if they haven't fully accepted the responsibility of their own spirituality, their faith is not their own. Many people like the idea of being "saved" and like to convey the image that they are righteous but putting in the actual work to apply it in their daily lives is still a struggle. It's a struggle for many of us.

You hear the Word, you read the Word, and you want to do right but wrong is still within you. Wrong is easier for you sometimes. Each day we are faced with choices, challenges, and decisions. It is up to each individual person how to react to every circumstance you are faced with. Be aware, no matter how spiritual you are, the devil will come for you.

For years, I've hosted a radio segment called "Relationship Hour." Through this platform, I've had the opportunity to speak with many men and women about a variety of topics. Although listeners get to hear many comments on air, it is those personal conversations off air that have touched my heart in several ways, and some of those situations have left me speechless.

I've talked with single women who only date men who have girlfriends and wives, because they believe this gives them the most benefits without the drawback of dealing with feelings and emotions. But some of those same women shed tears because deep down they want to be loved but can't find a man to care for them the same way they've seen men love others.

I've talked to women who have stayed in abusive relationships simply because they're afraid to leave and start over somewhere else. They've been degraded for so long that they've started to believe the belittling lies told by their spouses.

I've spoken with women who have been cheated on so many times they've started to cheat too as a way of getting revenge and dealing with the stress. I've spoken with both men and women who viewed their marriages as a business arrangement and were afraid to leave and tarnish the image they portrayed. I've even spoken with men who felt like they couldn't find a good, genuine woman to save their life.

You give life to things you entertain.

I've spoken with married couples, a man in particular, who experimented with threesomes in his marriage, and then left his wife for the woman they invited into the bedroom, whom he later married.

I've spoken with women who have experienced countless acts of betrayal. I've sat down with women who have had the courage and dignity to leave toxic relationships, only to have their spouse return as a supposedly repented, reformed man. I've talked to couples who have divorced twice and re-married three times!

New perspectives will give you new power.

Life can get hard, but you can get better. What do you do when the devil comes for you? You FIGHT. If you've taken to heart anything you've read here, fighting may now be easier. The things that bothered your spirit yesterday should not even be a part of your thought process today. Things you use to react to immediately should not even get a simple response. You give life to the things you entertain. Practice growing through everything you go through. Learn from every experience in your life and let your positive energy become contagious. New perspectives will give you new power.

Made in the USA
Columbia, SC
23 January 2021

31520736R00054